Afraid to Speak to Paid to Speak: How Overcoming Public Speaking Anxiety Boosts Your Confidence and Career

Lisa Ryan, MBA
Grategy ®

http://www.grategy.com

Copyright © 2013 Lisa Ryan

All Rights Reserved

All Rights Reserved.   No part of this book may be reproduced in any form or by any means without prior written permission of Lisa Ryan.

In other words, please play nice. Ask before you use, and then give proper attribution to the author. Thank You!

This book is dedicated to my wonderful husband Scott - I appreciate your amazing support and I love you more each day.

Table of Contents

It's time for you to shine 7
    Chapter Challenge: 10
    Notes: 11
CHAPTER ONE 13
If you fail to prepare, you prepare to fail 13
    Self-Assessment: 19
    Chapter Challenge: 21
    Notes: 22
CHAPTER TWO 23
To Learn by Heart or To Speak from the Heart? 23
    Self-Assessment: 26
    Chapter Challenge: 27
    Notes: 28
CHAPTER THREE 29
How to Find Friends and Appeal with Humor 29
    Self-Assessment: 33
    Chapter Challenge: 34
    Notes: 35
CHAPTER FOUR 37
Accept Your Imperfections 37
    Self-Assessment: 40
    Chapter Challenge: 41
    Notes: 42
CHAPTER FIVE 43
Pause Longer and Your Speech Will Prosper 43
    Self-Assessment: 46
    Chapter Challenge: 47
    Notes: 48
CHAPTER SIX 49
Act Confident and You'll Be Confident 49

    Self-Assessment: ...54

    Chapter Challenge ...55

    Notes: ...58

CHAPTER SEVEN ...59

Thank You - More Than Just a Last Remark ...59

    Self-Assessment: ...61

    Chapter Challenge: ...62

    Notes: ...63

CHAPTER EIGHT ...65

Give Yourself a Break ...65

    Self-Assessment: ...67

    Chapter Challenge: ...68

    Notes: ...69

CHAPTER NINE ...71

Choose Your Food and Drink Wisely ...71

    Self-Assessment: ...73

    Chapter Challenge: ...74

    Notes: ...75

CHAPTER TEN ...77

Dress Your Best for Speech Success ...77

    Self-Assessment: ...80

    Chapter Challenge: ...81

    Notes: ...82

It's Now Up to You ...83

    Self-Assessment: ...85

    Chapter Challenge: ...86

    Notes: ...87

References: ...89

About Lisa Ryan ...93

Other Books from Lisa Ryan: ...95

How to Keep in touch ...97

INTRODUCTION

It's time for you to shine

"There are always three speeches for every one you actually gave. The one you practiced, the one you gave, and the one you wish you gave" Dale Carnegie

Do you dream of having a career as a highly paid professional speaker? Perhaps you simply want to conduct a five-minute business presentation without embarrassing yourself. Either way, this e-book is for you!

Since you are reading this book, chances are that you are anxious about speaking to groups. What's the big deal? It's unlikely that you'll die on stage. Vaudeville actor George Jessel discloses what an amazing instrument the human brain is: "It starts working the moment you are born and never stops…until you stand up to speak in public." Stage fright feels like death, but it's certainly not fatal. So, why *do* most people fear speaking in public?

Comedian Jerry Seinfeld once said, "According to most studies, people's number one fear is public speaking. Number two is death. Death is number two. Does that sound right? This means to the average person, if you go to a funeral, you're better off in the casket than doing the eulogy."

According to thefreedictionary.com, *"glossophobia"* is the technical term describing a severe fear of public speaking. The word glossophobia comes from the Greek *glōssa*, meaning tongue, and *phobos*, meaning fear or dread. People who suffer from glossophobia tend to lose confidence or freeze in front of any audience, even if it's just a couple of people. They may experience physical symptoms like a dry mouth, weak voice, red face, sweating, trembling, and even heart palpitations. If you have suffered any of these signs of anxiety before or during a speech, this book is for you. We've identified the problem. Read on for the solution!

You'll find the techniques you need to successfully manage your fear in the following ten tips. Mind you, the word I use is "managing" your fear. As you'll learn from the stories and examples in this book, fear of speaking in public never *fully* goes away. If you're not at least a bit nervous, you may be getting complacent, and you don't want that!

Here are some of the statistics about public speaking: (1)

- People with speech anxiety: 74%

- Women with speech anxiety: 75 %

- Men with speech anxiety: 73%

As you can see, being afraid to speak in front of a group is pretty common! Here's the good news *and* the bad news about your nervousness: the bad news is that your tension probably will never entirely vanish. The good news is that by using these tips and techniques, along with lots of practice, you can manage your fear, boost your credibility, enhance your professional image, and elevate your career potential.

In this e-book, you'll find ideas from myriad professional speakers who share how they conquer their jitters. You'll also learn some best practices, and what can happen when those practices are not followed.

> Focus on the mission at hand. You are here to accomplish something requested of you. You were chosen to do this because you can.

Keynote speaker Steve Meyer summarizes the goal of a presentation: "Focus on the mission at hand. You are here to accomplish something requested of you. You were chosen to do this because you can. It is never about YOU (unless of course it is about you or your experiences or accomplishments). Always know where you're taking the audience from and to; be excited that you get to be the one to take them with you. Have your opening statements polished and thought provoking towards the mission at hand. When you lose sight of the mission or you are not prepared, the nerves kick in.

"When I am speaking, nobody has ever assaulted me, thrown stuff at me, or beat me up afterwards. The moral of the story: face your fears by charging onto that stage and giving the performance of your life!"

Let's explore how you can implement some basic strategies for overcoming anxiety with your very next talk. You'll reduce your nervousness to a manageable level and increase your ability to make a dynamic and well-received presentation.

Self-Assessment

Why do you want to improve your speaking skills?

_____

_____

_____

_____

_____

_____

What are you already doing well?

_____

_____

_____

_____

_____

What specific skills do you want to work develop when speaking in public?

_____

_____

_____

_____

_____

_____

Chapter Challenge:

List the organizations that you would ideally like to speak to.

Notes:

Notes:

CHAPTER ONE

If you fail to prepare, you prepare to fail

"There are no secrets to success. It is the result of preparation, hard work, and learning from failure." Colin Powell

If you want to be an effective public speaker, preparation is crucial. Remember, there is a reason you were asked to speak. In order to make the best impression possible, you must get ready. Start with information you are familiar with and use it to assemble your presentation. There are a variety of ways to get organized; just ask any speaker about the correct way to plan and you will find as many answers as you find speakers!

Michael Davis, a professional speaking coach, shares five questions to ask yourself as you get ready to speak. He learned them from his mentor, Darren LaCroix (a Toastmasters International World Champion of Public Speaking):

"1) What is my intent?

2) Am I present?

3) Will I have fun?

4) How would I give this presentation if I knew it would be the last one I ever give?"

Michael says, "This is a terrific process to help you focus attention where it needs to be - on your audience."

Give serious consideration to your **intent before** delivering your message. Consider how the information you plan to convey to your audience will affect them. In what ways will it benefit them? Do they need and want to know about this topic? What will they be able to do with what they have learned from you? Put your emphasis on asking these questions instead of covering every detail of the content of your speech.

Be **present**. Tune out distractions and turn off interrupters Avoid checking e-mail right before a speech, as tempting as that may be. A negative e-mail may take your mind off what you want to say. Power off your cell phone and put it away. In other words, give the audience your full attention.

Have **fun**. When you are having a good time, the audience senses it and they will enjoy your presentation more fully. We tend to take ourselves too seriously, always wanting to be the "expert." You can still be the expert with a smile!

Marketing professional, Brandi Starr continues to prepare all the way to her presentation. "In the car on the way to an event, I have a playlist that gets my energy flowing so that I'm pumped when I get there. I embrace my nerves. If I noticeably goof, I make a joke about it and keep going."

Some speakers take pride in being able to get up and "wing it." Even if you know your topic inside and out, ad-libbing can have detrimental effects. You may go off on a tangent, ramble, and even run out of time before you run out of material! You'll sound disorganized, and your points will be diluted if you haven't adequately prepared. Unplanned presentations lead to unsatisfied audiences.

A better approach is to learn to speak extemporaneously. Extemporaneous speaking differs from impromptu speaking in that you know your topic, practice what you're going to say, and deliver it in a way that doesn't *seem* rehearsed. Speaking extemporaneously sounds improvised, but you actually will have put a lot of time and effort into your preparing your presentation. Reaching this level of expertise takes practice, patience, and persistence. You will improve your skills each time you deliver a talk.

Ann Morris, an author and translator, says, "I do best when I'm speaking on a topic with which I have much experience and relevant anecdotes. People love to hear real examples, and they love to listen to an engaging teacher. I'm dedicated and excited about what I do.

> **Speak on a topic that you have experience and relevant anecdotes.**

They can see I'm relaxed and low-key with the audience. That makes them more comfortable. In short, I'm me talking about something I know and love. I share myself with my audience."

There are many tools available to make your speech preparation easier. In preparing for public speaking engagements, I like to entirely script my talk. I use a dictation software program called "Dragon Naturally Speaking" and simply "talk my talk." I use conversational language, and when it's done, it sounds like me! Perhaps you've heard speakers who wrote out their entire speech and delivered it verbatim; it sounded unnatural, didn't it? Aim to give a speech as though you are conversing with a friend. Dictation software is a terrific tool for that.

After dictating your speech, read it out loud at a normal speaking pace without stopping. There are several reasons to take this step. First, you want to hear how your speech *sounds*. Are you using big words that seem superfluous or awkward when said aloud? Replace them with simpler, more vibrant words.

Second, you should time your speech to see how long it will take you to deliver it. This gives you the opportunity to see if it will fit into the time allotted. If needed, you can then edit your speech to meet time specifications.

There will be many instances when you have a hard stop to your speech. If you go over, you risk having people leave before you've wrapped up your talk. Also, there are speaking events where timing truly is everything. For example, if you compete in a speech contest at a public speaking club such as Toastmasters International, you will be disqualified for going over/under time. Always err on the side of having less information than you need.

Small business owner Elliot Zovighian emphasizes proper speech prep. "I ensure I am extremely well researched, and rehearsed. I rehearse again, and then some more. I rehearse from the onset as if I was actually talking to my audience, with a voice full of inflection and pauses. I even attempt to anticipate interaction with questions and answers."

A little nervousness is perfectly normal for every presenter, but if you've done your homework and prepared well, you'll have the confidence you need to deliver your talk. Preparation can also help you deal with unexpected circumstances. Prepare a list called "What would I do if...?" Brainstorm everything that could go wrong during your talk. At a time when you are calm, cool, and collected, think about how you would handle each situation. Add to the list anytime you see or experience troubling situations. Review your list from time to time. It's like having your own fire drill - before an emergency happens.

Have a couple of "tricks up your sleeve" to be ready for unanticipated problems. If you are presenting a workshop, plan more activities than you think you will need. This comes in handy when you have an audience that does not like to participate, or you have more time than you originally planned. Then you can shorten or lengthen your program accordingly. Use the most relevant exercises first, but have extra activities available to add to the program if needed.

Just like the Boy Scout motto, "Be prepared." Bring extra batteries, markers, paper, and support materials with you. The batteries come in handy if a microphone fails in the middle of your presentation. Extra markers replace the dried-out ones. Carry extra handouts for unexpected attendees. These suggestions help you to control what you can control!

It is important to be done talking before the audience is done listening. Plan to have less material than needed to fill the time you've been allotted. Here are some guidelines: For a thirty-minute speech, prepare about twenty minutes of content. Thirty minutes of content will work for a forty-five minute speech, and if you have an hour, forty-five minutes of content is appropriate. You may need less material than these guidelines suggest in certain situations.

For example, say you are scheduled to finish a workshop at 10:00 a.m. When you wrap it up at 9:58; you're a hero, right? What happens if you're still speaking at 10:02? People are looking at their watches, packing up their belongings, and dashing out the door - without hearing any of your final comments or closing remarks. Stop when you're supposed to - better yet, end a few minutes early. Your audience will thank you for it.

When conducting my half-day presentation workshop, I have three and one-half hours available for the session, but I may only bring an hour and ten minutes worth of material. This allows time for the class to be highly interactive, yet there is enough content to help the participants understand what I am presenting. It makes the class about them, not about me.

What does having this additional time do for you? It gives you room to breathe. After all, how often have you tried to squeeze thirty minutes of content into a twenty minute time slot? If you've made the mistake of doing this, you've found that you speak too fast and fail to expand on the topics the audience wants to know more about. It may also torpedo your chance of a memorable conclusion, as you run out of time before you run out of material. By giving yourself leeway, you present your information at a reasonable speaking pace, allow for adequate pauses, and let the audience reflect on your message. This approach also allows the flexibility to answer questions or expand on certain points in more detail when you hit a hotspot for your audience.

If your program is running long, you may ask the audience for permission to exceed your time by a few minutes, but if there is a hard cutoff time, you should respect their wishes.

It is always better to edit your information than to speed up your recitation. If you begin with too much material, the process of editing will help you determine critical points to include. As you scrutinize your talk, assess the value of each point by asking yourself "Who cares?" If you cannot justify an idea, remove it. Whittle your talk down to the most significant topics by figuring out what the audience *needs* to hear, not what you *want* to tell them.

> As you scrutinize your talk, assess the value of each point by asking yourself "Who cares?" If you cannot justify an idea, remove it.

Once you have edited your talk to fit the time designated, reread it once or twice to get a feel for how it flows. Are there smooth transitions from topic to topic, or do you need to do some rearranging? If you haven't already worked personal stories into your talk, look for places that you can add clarity and punch with a story or anecdote.

Once you feel comfortable with the flow of the presentation and have read it several times, begin to reduce the talk to bullet points. Save the full script of your speech as a data file, and then choose "save as" for the bulleted version of the document.

Now, recite your speech again using only the outline. It is not going to be the same talk you just gave. Be okay with that. Every time you rehearse it, your speech will be slightly different.

After you've gone through your talk a few times using only the bullet points record it. Listen to the recording. Imagine that you are a member of your audience and decide if you like what you hear.

You'll find that you'll need to ignore how you sound. Most people don't like the sound of their own recorded voice. You are not listening to hear your voice per se; you are listening to discover the impact your vocal intonation has on your audience. Would you enjoy being a member of your own audience?

When you listen to a recording, write down the things that you like about your voice, as well as aspects that could be improved. You don't need to spend hours and hours doing this; a quick five to ten minute review of a session should give you an idea of what the rest of the recording reveals.

The recording gives you the opportunity to listen to yourself presenting your speech while you're driving or doing other tasks. It's a powerful tool to reinforce in your mind what you want to say.

When you've completed these steps, go through your speech one more time without any notes. Once again, it will be a slightly different speech, but by not using notes, you will be speaking more from the heart, and not so much from your head.

If you effectively *prepare* to speak, you will be much more relaxed in front of a group. Keep in mind, that even if you forget a significant chunk of what you were going to share, *the audience will have no idea what they missed*. If you missed an extremely salient point, find a way to circle back to it without apologizing or tipping off the audience to your mistake.

When you apologize to an audience, you reduce their perception of your credibility. This is not to suggest that you would never answer, "I don't know," to a question; you always have that option. "No apologies" means that you never start your talk with an apology; i.e. not having enough time, forgetting what you were going to say, losing your place, or not having enough information.

Remember, you offer knowledge and expertise that someone believes is beneficial to an audience. That is your strength. There will always be people that know more than you do, and people that know less than you do. Your job is to do the best you can with what you have, and preparing for your talk will make a difference.

Self-Assessment:

What topic(s) would you like to speak about? What benefits will your audience gain from your talk? (Entertainment, knowledge, inspiration, personal development…)

_____
_____
_____
_____
_____
_____
_____

How can you make sure that you are fully present for your audience?

_____
_____
_____
_____
_____
_____
_____

How will you make your speech fun for yourself and for others?

_____
_____
_____
_____
_____
_____
_____

How would you give this presentation if you knew it would be the last one you ever give?"

_____
_____
_____
_____
_____

What is your presentation "Plan B"?

_____
_____
_____
_____
_____

What can you do to make sure you are prepared?

_____
_____
_____
_____
_____

Chapter Challenge:

Choose at least one of the organizations you listed in the last challenge and brainstorm ideas for specific topics to speak to them about:

Notes:

CHAPTER TWO

To Learn by Heart or To Speak from the Heart?

"It's fun being able to suit up and go and kick butt and not have to worry about memorizing dialogue. It's a whole different way of acting because you're not depending on the words at all; you're really depending on everything else that you have." Kelly Hu

In the last chapter, we explored the value of preparing to speak. You may be wondering "Rather than rehearse my speech over and over and have it come out differently every time, why don't I just memorize it?" The definition of the word memorize is to "commit to memory or to learn by heart."(2) Although you don't want to commit a speech to memory, you do want to learn to talk from your heart. Share what you know, and don't be overly concerned about putting the words in a particular order.

In the section on preparation, you learned that I like to script my talks. Again, I do not recommend memorizing your talk. Several unfortunate things may happen if you rely on your memory:

   1) You draw a complete blank: your speech disappears from your memory bank and you have no way to access your "mental files."

   2) Your talk will sound memorized and stilted to your audience.

   3) You won't have the flexibility to add relevant anecdotes or to ask for feedback from the audience.

I suggest that you "bookend" your speech by memorizing your opening and closing statements. This will help you to start off strong. Stuttering or hesitating on your opening point will detract from how powerfully you come across. A persuasive ending that has been committed to memory adds power to your conclusion.

Captivating your audience in your first few seconds on stage is crucial to the success of your speech. Don't start with "Today I'm going to tell you…" Just tell them! Some ways to get your audience involved from the beginning of your talk are to:

- State a startling statistic
- Ask a rhetorical question
- Tell a funny story
- Share a quote or poem

Practice your opening line so often that if someone were to shake you awake from a deep sleep and ask for your opening line you would be able to deliver it. Your audience's first impression of you can make or break your entire presentation.

Remember to be consistent throughout your presentation. If you open with a hilarious story, the audience is going to expect at least some humor during the course of your talk. Loop your ending back to your opening story. This technique brings your presentation to a close and gives the audience a sense of completion.

If you use note cards, make sure that you number them. That way if you drop them, you can easily put them back in order. Keep your notes brief, using only bullet points or key words. If you are referring to a note card to recite a quote, make sure that you have read the quote so frequently that you are familiar with the message. That way, you can maintain your connection with the audience instead of looking down at your notes.

> **If you use note cards, make sure that you number them. That way if you drop them, you can easily put them back in order.**

Occasionally you may be required to read a script verbatim. If so, make sure that you review the text so thoroughly that all you need to do is glance down to find your spot. As much as you are able to, keep eye contact with members of your audience. When you're reading a script, you not only lose your connection with the audience, your voice projects into the lectern instead of out to the audience. This can make it difficult for you to be heard and understood.

Know your conclusion so well it also rolls off your tongue. By leaving your audience inspired, energized, and feeling good, you create lasting positive perception of you and your topic. End strong. After all, the last words you say are probably going to be the ones your audience most remembers. There are many ways to close a speech. A few examples are: the moral of the story, a call to action, or an inspirational poem or quote. By ensuring that your opening and closing are strong, you have a lot of flexibility for the body of your speech.

When you know your information well, you know it well enough to present. Trust yourself and speak from your heart.

Self-Assessment:

What are some of the ways you will open your speech?

_____
_____
_____
_____
_____
_____
_____

Write down some potential closes for your speech?

_____
_____
_____
_____
_____
_____
_____

What relevant anecdotes or stories will you share?

_____
_____
_____
_____
_____

Chapter Challenge:
Create a title for your talk and a brief description of your three key points:

Notes:

CHAPTER THREE

How to Find Friends and Appeal with Humor

"Humor is a universal language." Unknown

Arrive early so that you can meet the attendees as they enter the meeting room. Smile, shake hands and introduce yourself to as many people as possible. Ask what they are expecting from your talk, and see if they have any questions before you begin. Learn the names of at least a few people and, when appropriate, refer to them throughout your talk.

Speaker and author Laurie Westphal shares her best tip for finding a friend: "I walk around the room and strike up a conversation with at least three or four people about different topics. Maybe they're holding a big drink. I'll say, 'Stocking up on caffeine huh?', or my favorite - when they are scoping out the entire handout before we start, I will say 'I am glad you are going through that, now I can go home, and you can do the session!' No matter what it is, it is usually something that makes us both laugh. This makes me feel more confident, and since I have already shared a smile with some people in the crowd if I start to feel nervous, I just look their way and smile - they usually smile back."

Professional speaker and trainer, Kimberley Richardson overcomes nervousness with practice and visualization. "As a professional speaker, I recognize first that I am delivering a message that should respect and honor my audiences. Hours of prep go into every engagement - even if I have delivered it 100 times.

"During this process, I imagine my audiences' reactions to every word spoken and story shared. When I arrive at the hotel the night before, I go into the room I will be speaking in to familiarize myself with the room layout. The morning of the engagement, I get there early to shake hands and introduce myself to as many as people as possible - before I speak. This way, I feel I have made some genuine connections with people - they see me as approachable and give back through their attentiveness. Paying them in advance to smile and applaud wouldn't hurt either, but so far I have refrained from doing so!"

Even if you know only two or three people in your audience, no matter what size it is, use their names. This will make your audience believe that you care enough to get to know them, and it also creates a sense of engagement with them. The other advantage of using names throughout the presentation is that it keeps people on their toes. If you are asking questions or using names, there is less of a chance that members of your audience will check their smart phones or chat with friends. After all, no one wants to get "busted" checking their e-mails during a talk.

As you introduce yourself to people, look specifically for friendly people, those that are excited to be there, are interested in your topic and have a positive aura. Make eye contact with them throughout your talk. By concentrating on welcoming faces, you will feel more confident and build rapport.

> By concentrating on welcoming faces, you will feel more confident and build rapport.

No matter how many smiling faces you have in your audience, there probably will be one or two people that, for whatever reason, aren't happy to be there. Don't let them bother you. Chances are that they are not upset with you. I learned this lesson during a talk for a civic organization where the average age was 70 years old.

One woman in the group had her arms folded and was glaring at me during my entire presentation. No matter what I did, I could not get her to smile. The rest of the room was having a fabulous time and was highly engaged in the information I was presenting, but I kept coming back to that one ill-tempered woman. It turned out that she was nearly deaf, and the expression on her face was from her straining to hear what I had to say. I made a judgment based on an incorrect assumption; and I may have lessened the power of my talk by focusing all of my energy on getting her to smile.

If you are giving a presentation to an audience that has been "sentenced" to attend, you will find at least a few responsive people. Locate them. Your opening remarks and the content of your speech may gradually woo over the others, but by doing this you will boost your sense of confidence.

Those in your audience want to like you. The best way to build immediate rapport with them is to smile. Make a connection, engage your audience and *smile*. Even if you are addressing a serious topic, at some point you'll want to elevate the mood of your audience.

You may be thinking, "But Lisa, the information that I present could not be more boring and dry. How can I possibly make it fun or funny?" Take the time to review your talk and find places to inject humor. Incorporate personal stories. Share unexpected twists that arose while compiling your research or interviewing your subjects. Add a little self-deprecating humor. The stories do not have to be uproarious; look for little idiosyncrasies that add some amusement.

Remember a time when you sat through a painfully dry educational session based on stale facts and tedious figures. You're probably cringing right now. Isn't it true that the moment a presenter shares a personal story you sit up, lean forward, and pay attention? We live in a "National Enquirer" society. We are curious about other people. What makes them tick? What interests them? What have they experienced? When a presenter shares a personal experience, the audience feels more connected and engaged with the speaker. Make sure you add a slice of your own life for the enjoyment of your audience.

> When a presenter shares a personal experience, the audience feels more connected and engaged with the speaker.

Sprinkling humor in your talk does not mean you must tell jokes. If you have a joke that fits in with your topic, *and* you are a good storyteller, feel free to use it. However, if there is any question at all about how this joke will go over with your audience, either eliminate it or ask the person who requested that you speak if they feel the joke is appropriate. Never use off-color jokes, ethnic jokes, or foul language within your jokes. No matter how well you know your audience, you risk offending someone, reducing your credibility, and potentially getting yourself into enormous trouble.

After writing your speech, review it, looking for specific areas where you can add witticisms. If you are not naturally funny, share your idea of the speech with a hilarious friend and ask for suggestions for adding more humor. Adding jest may take you out of your comfort zone. Straying from your comfort zone is suitable, but be careful not to go so far that you feel anxious, because your audience will sense your anxiety. Allow yourself to relax and have fun, and the audience will have fun too.

As you gradually add humor to your presentations, it becomes easier. Before long you will master this skill. There are plenty of books on the subject of humor in public speaking, with easy-to-learn techniques that can instantly make you funnier. When something funny happens, write it down. By keeping a humor journal, you will be able to access humorous stories of your own to share.

A great way to add humor is to use a "call-back." A call-back is a phrase or part of a story that you refer to throughout your talk. If you're using a funny call-back, every time you utter it, your audience will laugh.

Call-backs are also a terrific way to close a speech. By using the circular technique of the call-back, you let your audience know that the speech is complete by bringing them back to the place where it started.

When you look for ways to lighten up your speech with humor, both you and your audience will enjoy the experience even more.

Self-Assessment:

What can you do to connect with your audience?

_____
_____
_____
_____
_____
_____
_____

What funny stories can you add to your talk?

_____
_____
_____
_____
_____
_____
_____

What call-backs can you refer to throughout your speech?

_____
_____
_____
_____
_____
_____
_____

Chapter Challenge:

Script your phone call. Write down what you will say when you call an organization to present yourself as a potential speaker for an upcoming event.

Notes:

Notes:

CHAPTER FOUR

Accept Your Imperfections

"My imperfections and failures are as much a blessing from God as my successes and my talents and I lay them both at his feet." Mahatma Gandhi

Believe it or not, your audience is much more forgiving of your speaking errors than you might think. We all want to be dynamic presenters. We desire to be seen as an expert based on the information we provide during our session. In fact, we want to be perfect. Sound familiar? Get over it. One of the nice things about the idea of being perfect is that nobody is.

Motivational speaker Glenda Watson Hyatt has cerebral palsy, which makes her head-control tenuous. She addresses this right away in her opening by saying, "I'd also like to mention that when some people are nervous their faces turn beet red, when I'm nervous my head bobs for apples. The fact that you cannot see the apples makes me question which one of us has the disability." Her openness about her disability gets the audience to laugh and immediately puts them at ease.

Freelance journalist and translator Annalisa Dolzan divulges, "Once I learned to feel comfortable inside my own skin, I let my energy flow and fill my body, and I relax. I also feel comfortable in my persona, aware but not scared of showing my weaknesses and flaws, as well as my strong points."

Ms. Dolzan feels that people are ill at ease while speaking because they feel exposed, "as if they became suddenly and helplessly aware of what they don't like about themselves and anxious everybody will notice that. Accepting one's flaws and looks is the key, along with deep, relaxing breathing."

Don't strive for perfection; aim for excellence. The more prepared you are for the unexpected, the better your talk will be. If everything were to go exactly according to plan every time you spoke, how would you learn? You improve by making mistakes, fixing them, and moving forward. Of course, you want to give your audience your best, but when something goes wrong, the key to success is: "Never let them see you sweat."

I was conducting a lengthy presentations skills class for a room full of high school students. I began the class by addressing their fear of public speaking. I asked them what they have seen happen to others, or what they had experienced while making a presentation. There were a variety of responses: sweating, stuttering, losing your place, looking down, speaking too fast, racing heart and more.

As I was creating the list, I tripped and fell. This was not a graceful fall. One moment I was standing up, and the next I was flat on the ground. Extremely embarrassed, but not wanting them to see me sweat, I brushed myself off, picked up the pile of papers that were strewn across the floor, and added "trip" to the list. After assuring everyone that I was alright, I continued the session.

When I shared this incident later that day, I was asked if the students thought that it was part of my routine. It would have been an Oscar-winning level performance to pull that one off. In hindsight, I was glad that the fall happened (and I didn't get hurt). It gave the students the opportunity to see what to do when something goes incredibly wrong in a presentation. No matter what happens during the course of your presentation, you must proceed. How smoothly you overcome unexpected obstacles affects the success of your talk.

When something odd happens during your presentation, you have two options: you can ignore it, or you can address the situation (without apology). For example, if the room is exceptionally hot or frigidly cold, let your audience know that you are aware of the situation, and you are seeing what can be done to resolve it. If a light is flickering, or you're having technical difficulties, lighten the atmosphere with humor. When you feel stressed, you convey those feelings of anxiety to your audience. When you handle a problem without losing your composure, you are not only showing your professionalism, you are also letting others know that it's okay when things go wrong.

> When something odd happens during your presentation, you have two options: you can ignore it, or you can address the situation (without apology).

You probably have your own stories of situations that arose during presentation due to circumstances outside of your control. Here are some of the unfortunate incidents I have survived to talk about:

- Having to describe each slide in picturesque detail when the projector malfunctioned for a PowerPoint presentation

- A group evacuation down twenty-three flights of steps when a fire alarm sounded in the middle of a training class

- A dog walked into the room to visit its owner. The dog happened to be a little gassy, and his noxious odor nearly asphyxiated us

You will encounter ringing cell phones, technology failures and a host of other disturbances. Things go wrong, and it's up to you to handle it as best as you can. Ultimately, only you and the quality of your talk are under your control.

Speaking coach, Sally Raymond sums up the art of accepting your imperfections: "As a speaker, you have to get comfortable with being uncomfortable. You have to be willing to put yourself in those situations where you have to perform. For me, my comfort level with speaking changed when I changed my perspective. When I first began to give presentations, I was very focused on myself: Will they notice me shaking? Will my mouth get pitchy because I'm so nervous? Will I freeze up and forget everything? The list went on and on.

"After several years of this agony, I finally discovered how to shift my mindset. I began to take the focus away from myself and focus instead on what I wanted my audience to take away from my presentation. This simple shift in my thinking has made a huge impact on how comfortable I feel when I'm speaking. Now I am able to focus on my audience and how my message will serve them."

Self-Assessment:

What has gone wrong (or what do you imagine can go wrong) during a speech?

_____
_____
_____
_____
_____
_____
_____

How could you have handled (or how would you handle) the situation differently?

_____
_____
_____
_____
_____
_____
_____

How will you improve your talk for next time?

_____
_____
_____
_____
_____
_____
_____

Chapter Challenge:

Call the organizations you would like to speak to, using the script that you wrote (and practiced.) Call until you receive three "No's" or one "Yes" for you to speak. (Although you will probably start out speaking for free, if someone offers you a fee, feel free to take it - and celebrate!)

Notes:

CHAPTER FIVE

Pause Longer and Your Speech Will Prosper

"The most precious things in speech are pauses" Ralph Richardson

No matter how long you have been speaking and how talented you are, it's likely that your talk can benefit from more pauses. When you are nervous, your tendency is to speak more quickly than normal, spewing out as much information as you can in the shortest possible time so you can escape the stage. When you fail to take a breath, you are not benefitting your audience, nor are you helping yourself. Deep breathing keeps you calm, makes your voice more resonant, and gives the audience the time to consider what you just said.

Pausing is hard to do, because most people dislike silence. We try to fill every iota of silence with sound, using connector words such as "like," "but," and "or," and sprinkling "ah's" and "um's" throughout our presentation. You do not impress your audience with a litany of non-words. Pausing between sentences help you start each sentence with a "real" word.

If you are presenting a technical, financial, or clinical talk, you may be using words that are unfamiliar to your audience. Make sure that you stay away from industry jargon, as there may be people who don't understand. If you have to use an acronym, make sure you explain the acronym the first time you say it. You'll find that acronyms mean different things to different audiences, so make sure they know what you mean.

If your audience loses their train of thought because you are speaking too fast and not pausing to let them process your information, they will never catch up with you. Our minds are designed to process information as we hear it. By using strategic pauses, you allow your audience to keep pace with you. It may feel like a pause lasts forever, but your audience will feel better because you stopped talking for a moment. They are able to relax and sort out the information that you are presenting.

You add credibility when you stop talking, instead of using a connector word such as "and," "or," "but," or "like." The best place to insert a pause is at a point of punctuation. Simply use a period to end the sentence and stop speaking. Using too many connector words creates one long sentence, making it difficult for the audience to comprehend your point. Vary the length of your sentences. Changing sentence length adds interest and keeps the audience engaged.

{ **Changing sentence length adds interest and keeps the audience engaged.** }

Pausing also helps with your storytelling. Imagine that you are sharing a funny incident with a friend. Do you recite "just the facts" without emotion, or do you add humor and drama to bring the story to life? Do you incorporate a dramatic pause before sharing the unexpected ending? Yes, chances are that you do all of this naturally in your personal conversations. Using these same skills adds life to your presentations as well.

Just like the end-of-season cliffhanger of a television series, you should linger before concluding. Then, when you've shared your surprise ending, give the audience the appropriate amount of time to digest what you just told them. Sometimes it takes a moment or two to truly "get" the story.

Make sure you pause for laughter. When you share a funny story, or tell a joke, give your audience the opportunity to enjoy and experience the emotions of happiness, laughter, and fun. There are many times when "step on the laughter," by continuing to speak before your audience is done laughing. When your audience laughs, you can be sure that they are enjoying themselves, and that is a gift. Let them relish the moment.

In addition to laughter, use the pause to take your audience on an emotional roller coaster. When you are telling a story that has serious implications, pause to let the audience absorb the direness of the situation. When you are sharing something sad, allow them to feel the sadness. Of course, you never want to leave your audience on a down note. Look for ways to elevate the mood so they leave feeling better than when they arrived.

The pause not only serves the audience, it serves you, the speaker. Pausing gives you the opportunity to collect your thoughts before proceeding. It's not necessary to make any sound while you are thinking. Again, using filler words like "ah" or "um" distracts the audience and does not benefit you.

Look for opportunities to use an extended pause to collect your thoughts. When you are walking from one side of the podium to the other, occasionally do so silently. If you are using PowerPoint and forget what you're going to say, or don't know what is on the screen behind you, take a breath, turn around silently and walk towards the screen, reading as you go. When you get to the screen, simply point to something that you want to emphasize, and walk back towards the audience. Although you may feel silly being quiet, and a pause may feel like an eternity, your audience appreciates them and needs them.

The next time you sit through a presentation, pay attention to how the speaker uses pauses. Start to get a feel for what works-what you like, and what feels right to you. Look for approaches that work as well as those that don't work or make you feel uncomfortable. In addition to taking notes on content, take notes on the skill and style of the presenter. The more you are aware of what others are doing, the easier it will be for you to develop your skills. Do *not* imitate another speaker; your goal is to be the most authentic *you* possible, not a poor replica of someone else.

> Do *not* imitate another speaker; your goal is to be the most authentic *you* possible, not a poor replica of someone else.

Pausing is an easy tool to use, and extraordinarily effective in delivering a message with impact, emotion, and credibility. Pausing allows your audience to keep pace with you and better understand the information that you are presenting.

Self-Assessment:

What do you notice about people who effectively use pausing while speaking?

_____
_____
_____
_____
_____
_____
_____
_____

Why do you feel it's difficult to pause during a speech?

_____
_____
_____
_____
_____
_____
_____
_____

How will you remind yourself to pause?

_____
_____
_____
_____
_____
_____
_____
_____

Chapter Challenge:

Develop an outline for your speech. Write down your three key points and at least one story/anecdote for each point.

Notes:

CHAPTER SIX

Act Confident and You'll Be Confident

"Our deepest fear is not that we are inadequate. Our deepest fear is that we are powerful beyond measure. It is our light, not our darkness, that frightens us most. We ask ourselves, 'Who am I to be brilliant, gorgeous, talented, and famous?' Actually, who are you not to be?"
Marianne Williamson

It's time for a little experiment. Whatever you are doing right now, assume the posture of a depressed person. What just happened to your body? Where are your shoulders? Are you standing tall or slouching? Where are you gazing? Are you looking straight ahead, or looking down? Is your breathing strong and deep, or short and shallow? It's a good bet that your shoulders are slumping, you're looking down, and your breathing is shallow. You may even start to hear negative self-talk in this position. If you stay this way long enough, there's a good chance that no matter what your mood was before, it's a little less upbeat now.

Now assume the posture of the most confident person on the planet. Ask yourself the same questions. Where are your shoulders? Where are you gazing? How is your breathing? You'll probably find that your shoulders are back, your spine is straight and tall, you're looking forward or looking up, your breath is deep and strong, and you feel more upbeat than you were just a moment ago.

Our physical state makes all the difference in how we feel about ourselves and how others perceive us. Motivational guru Tony Robbins says, "Change your physiology; change your state." It's true. Just by taking a strong physical stance, we feel better and more confident than we would otherwise.

Pay close attention to both your physical stance and your mental attitude. You have several choices before you begin speaking: you could pace nervously back and forth, looking down and thinking, "I am going to be horrible. I am very nervous. People are going to know that I am a fraud. Why am I here? I don't have anything important to say." You could work yourself into such a tizzy that it will feel as if every single one of those negative affirmations are coming true.

Instead, you could "lie" to yourself and change your attitude. As you wait for your turn to speak, stand tall, with your shoulders back and your gaze forward. Smile. Take a deep breath. Inhale, and feel your chest and stomach expand. Allow the oxygen to reach your extremities. Now release your breath slowly. Take a few more deep breaths, and relax.

Speaker and author, VJ Sleight, shares how she relieves her stress before a presentation: "Deep and slow breathing will slow the heart rate which will lower anxiety. The breath cycle should be for 10 seconds. I also will place on my hands on the floor (I'm extremely flexible) and let the blood run to my brain."

> Deep and slow breathing will slow the heart rate which will lower anxiety. The breath cycle should be for 10 seconds.

Brandi Starr also uses breathing techniques to relax before her talks: "Breathing works for me. I take a moment backstage or in a restroom to close my eyes and take slow deep breaths. I picture myself delivering my presentation, being absolutely amazing and the crowd totally engaged."

After breathing deeply, fill your mind with positive self-talk. Even if you don't believe it at first, say to yourself, "I am going to rock this presentation! I have the knowledge, skills, and ability to give my audience the information that they need. I am confident, my audience likes me, and I like them." Find the words that can make you feel strong, powerful, confident, and well-liked by your audience; then, use those words. At first your subconscious may fight you. Every time it kicks in with a negative comment, simply say, "Cancel, cancel, cancel." Over time, you will find this practice easier to do.

Speaker, trainer and consultant Lorraine Arams divulges a straightforward technique that works for her every time. She says, "When I feel the nervousness I simply repeat to myself: 'I am, I can, I will.' It seems to calm the mind like a mantra."

Think about two speakers: the best one you have ever witnessed and one who was not particularly good. Picture how each one carried himself or herself. What was his posture like? Did she apologize for her lack of preparation? Did he approach the lectern calmly and confidently and smile at the crowd? Did she make strong eye contact? Resolve to mimic the behavior of the better of the two. Remember that even the most confident speakers have to battle their nerves each and every time they take the stage. Nervousness never fully goes away.

CEO Henry Hutchins discloses, "The times I was not nervous were the times I did a poor job. I just acknowledge the butterflies in my stomach, get them into formation, and proceed." Keep in mind that you are nervous because you care about doing a good job, not because you are unworthy, ill-prepared or unqualified to speak. With practice and positive self-talk, you will be on the road to a successful speech.

Phillip Gary Smith is a speaker who has an intriguing way of looking at butterflies, "A breakthrough for me was when I understood the feeling of 'butterflies.' They're not 'nervousness' showing up, but rather due to the blood traveling from the abdomen to other parts of the body that need the supply. For example, if one were competing in a foot-race, the blood would be heading to muscles. Now I acknowledge them, knowing it's the body's way of announcing it is getting ready to perform whether speaking or competing."

Two of the most powerful confidence-building concepts are to remember that the audience has no idea what you're going to tell them, and that they don't see your nervousness. Why are these ideas important? As a speaker, you know what you want to say. You alone know the statistics, stories, and examples you plan to share throughout your talk. Although you carry the information in your mind, the audience has no idea what you plan to say. If you skip a story, they won't know. If you neglect to mention a vital statistic, they won't know that either. If you need to, circle back to that point when you remember to do so.

> **Two of the most powerful confidence-building concepts are to remember that the audience has no idea what you're going to tell them, and that they don't see your nervousness.**

Sometimes we get so caught up in our topic that we feel everything has to be perfect, and that the audience will know when we've skipped something. They won't. Nor will they be aware of the level of anxiety you may be experiencing. If you notice a quiver in your voice or your hand shaking, the audience will likely not detect it, or at worst, they will overlook it.

Next, remind yourself that the audience does not see signs of nervousness. Although you feel like your heart is about to beat its way out of your chest, a pool of sweat is forming below your dripping palms, and fainting is a likely occurrence, the audience won't see any of that. There are a few situations in which the audience may see that you are nervous. If you are holding a piece of paper, it may rustle. If your face turns the color of a beet, or splotches mysteriously appear on your neck, they will notice that! Otherwise, they won't be aware of how anxious you feel.

At my niece's wedding reception, it was the best man's turn to toast the newly-married couple. His talk was written out on several sheets of paper, and as he started to read, his hands shook violently, rustling the paper loudly. If I had simply been listening to his voice, I would never have known that he was petrified. But I could see and hear the paper shaking. A better approach would have been to hold index cards instead of paper. Then, he could have referred to his notes without tipping off the audience to his nervousness.

I remember the first time that I made a presentation at my chapter's meeting of the National Speakers Association. I longed to make a good impression, but I was terrified. At one point, I lifted my right arm toward the ceiling to emphasize a point. As I looked up, I saw my hand shaking. After only a moment, I lowered my hand. Chances are that most people in the room did not notice that little flutter, and I survived. Now, even though I'm initially uneasy when speaking in front of my peers, I no longer shake.

Keynote speaker and trainer John Rasiej shares how he grounds himself and captures his energy before a talk: "I imagine roots coming down from my feet, digging down for the energy of the earth. Once I feel those roots, I visualize the roots turning every color I can imagine and vacuum them up into my body, placing them somewhere I can access those swirling colors when it comes time to start the speech." He continues, "Once you've practiced this, it's an exercise that can be done in the blink of an eye, so you can use it to re-ground yourself in the middle of a speech if you feel you've lost focus."

Confidence comes with practice; the more talks you give, the more confident you become. I gave my first speech, called the "Icebreaker "when I joined a Toastmasters club in 1987. If you're not familiar with Toastmasters International, it is a public speaking organization that was founded in 1924 to help members improve their communication, public speaking and leadership skills.

The Icebreaker is a four- to six-minute speech that allows the speaker to introduce themselves to the club. I called my speech "Accessories, the Key to Life." It was a subject I knew well - me and my love of accessorizing my outfits. I shook for a full half-hour before my talk… and for 45 minutes more afterwards. However, as I continued making speeches to the club, I became less nervous.

After several years in Toastmasters, I left the club because I thought I had outgrown it. After all, I was presenting regularly, and thought I was doing well. One night, I was asked to introduce a speaker at a seminar. I approached the stage, said a few words, and drew a blank as I attempted to introduce my friend. As I sat down next to my husband Scott, I was trembling. He asked me, "What is wrong with you?" My only response to him was, "I need to go back to Toastmasters." I knew that I needed to keep up with the regular practice in a safe environment that Toastmasters offered me.

If you want to learn more about Toastmasters International, make sure you visit their website at: http://www.toastmasters.org. You can find a club in your area and begin to develop the skills you need to increase your confidence and your expertise when speaking to a group. An investment of one hour a week to attend a meeting will have a significant impact on the quality of your speaking.

Ask Mary Kay Ash once said, "Fake it until you make it." The more confident you act, over time the more confident you will be.

Self-Assessment:

How does your physiology change when you change your state?

_____
_____
_____
_____
_____
_____
_____

What breathing techniques work best for you?

_____
_____
_____
_____
_____
_____
_____

How does knowing the audience can't see your nervousness help you?

_____
_____
_____
_____
_____
_____
_____

Chapter Challenge

Write out your speech in full. Read it out loud to make sure it sounds like you. Time yourself to see how long it takes to read it at a conversational pace. (Use extra paper if needed)

_____
_____
_____
_____
_____
_____
_____
_____
_____
_____
_____
_____
_____
_____
_____
_____
_____
_____
_____
_____
_____
_____
_____
_____
_____

Notes:

CHAPTER SEVEN

Thank You - More Than Just a Last Remark

"To speak gratitude is courteous and pleasant, to enact gratitude is generous and noble, but to live gratitude is to touch Heaven."
Johannes A. Gaertner

Your audience can tell whether you like them or not. No matter how you act, if you are not sincere your audience will know it. Do you believe you're not as good or as talented as those in your audience? They will perceive your lack of confidence. Do you feel that you're better than your audience? They will sense your condescending attitude. Do you love your audience and feel excited to be with them? They will feel that too.

Begin your talk by immersing yourself in positive feelings towards your audience. Although you may not like everything about everyone, observe as many positive attributes as possible before approaching the stage. Find encouragement in the energy of the group, the cause which you are supporting, or the information that you will present. Are you glad you didn't have to travel, or excited that you are speaking in a brand-new venue? Is this your first paid speaking engagement or will you be receiving your full fee? Write it all down. Listing what you're grateful for increases your positive feelings toward the audience and makes them feel more connected to you.

If you are not familiar with making a gratitude list, it's a remarkably simple process. Sit down with a pen and paper, and visualize your audience. Begin to write down everything positive you can think of about those who will attend your talk. If you don't know your audience members particularly well, or you can't picture them, make up a favorable response. Write down everything you would like to believe about your audience. It may sound corny, but it works.

If you want to not only overcome your fear of speaking, but improve the quality in all areas of your life, a gratitude journal may help you. Although it sounds like a time-consuming process, a gratitude journal takes less than five minutes a day to complete. After you get up or before you go to bed, write down three to five items for which you are grateful. Start each sentence with "I am grateful for..." Challenge yourself to come up with as many different items as you can and also to add detail to each of them. For example, instead of writing, "I am grateful for my client," I write, "I am grateful that my client made a special effort to remember my birthday with a beautiful card." Each time you write a sentence, inject as much emotion into it as you can. Feel grateful and experience the emotion of appreciation once you've written it down.

What does a gratitude journal have to do with overcoming anxiety in public speaking? A lot. When you take the time to appreciate what you have, you become more confident and have a more positive outlook.

> **When you take the time to appreciate what you have, you become more confident and have a more positive outlook.**

After your talk, make sure you send thank-you notes to the meeting organizer and anyone else who helped you with the event. A handwritten note is best. Keep a stash of notecards, pens and stamps in your car. At the end of an engagement, while you're still in the parking lot, write a quick note and pop it in the mailbox on your way home. Talk about making an impression! This habit will help keep you in top-of-mind awareness the next time that organization needs a professional speaker.

Besides using "snail mail," you may choose to use online services such as SendOutCards or any of myriad sites that allow you to create your own cards. See if you can get a picture of yourself at the event, perhaps even with the organizer. Upload this picture to the front of the card and write a personal note of thanks. Your card will be delivered by the online service, making it unnecessary to buy stamps or go to the post office to send it.

As author Gladys Brown Stern says, "Silent gratitude isn't much use to anyone." Express your appreciation to your audience before, during, and after your program. In return, they will thank you with positive feedback and referrals!

Self-Assessment:

What are you grateful for about your audience?

_____
_____
_____
_____
_____
_____
_____
_____

How will you express your appreciation to your audience?

_____
_____
_____
_____
_____
_____
_____
_____

Why is gratitude good before, during and after a speech?

_____
_____
_____
_____
_____
_____
_____
_____

Chapter Challenge:

Now that you've written out your speech, condense it down to bullet points (or notecards) and practice the speech using just your notecards. Time yourself to see how long you take to give the talk.

Notes:

Notes:

CHAPTER EIGHT

Give Yourself a Break

"Luck is what happens when preparation meets opportunity." Seneca

When you feel tired or rushed, you will not be at your best for your presentation. It's vital to get at least seven hours of sleep every night, and this is particularly beneficial the night before a big presentation. Go to bed early, setting your alarm so you have plenty of time to complete everything you need to accomplish before your presentation. Early to bed and early to rise, makes a speaker healthy, wealthy and wise.

Do as much as you can the night before your session. Make a list of everything you need to bring, and physically check off each item as you put it in your car.

If you're using PowerPoint, make sure you have your presentation on both your laptop and a flash drive as a backup. There will be times when your computer is not compatible with the available equipment. A flash drive generally solves any problems with incompatibility.

Arrive at your destination at least an hour before your starting time. This will give you the opportunity to test equipment, set out your handouts, get a feel for the room, and take a breath before your guests arrive. Nothing is worse than scurrying around, frantically trying to get everything done at the last minute.

There will always be a few early arrivals. When you are set up and ready to go, spend a few minutes with those early birds. Learn something about them and ask what's on their mind. Not only does this practice give you a friendly face or two to find in the crowd, they may also share relevant stories that you can incorporate in your talk.

Have a few prepared questions to ask attendees when you meet them. For example, "If I could wave a magic wand and give you exactly what you expect out of this session, what would it be?" Or "What attracted you to this session today?" Use open-ended questions that will give you some insight as to the makeup and mindset of your participants. Stay away from the cliché, "So, what do you do?" A better question is,

"What do you do when you're not working?" Your ability to work audience feedback into your talk endears you to your audience.

Ken Grant, a project manager and consultant, reveals how he prepares for his talks: "1.) Don't overthink it. Before a presentation, I make sure my rehearsals and prep are complete well I begin. Then I spend the time (likely to be several hours) thinking or doing anything that will keep my mind off the presentation. 2.) You are the expert or you wouldn't be on the stage. Part of my preparation is anticipating what questions this group is likely to ask, so I can have prepared responses for questions or hecklers. 3.) Have a mantra. I keep repeating, to myself, 'Confidence and Enthusiasm.' If I know the material and have prepared, I only need to deliver it with confidence and enthusiasm."

Always remember: no matter how many circumstances you can control, there will always be situations that you cannot control. When you arrive early, meet people, and have a contingency plan for unexpected circumstances, you will do your best, and the audience will appreciate your efforts.

Self-Assessment:

Why is it important not to overthink your talk?

_____
_____
_____
_____
_____
_____
_____
_____

What questions are your audiences most likely to ask?

_____
_____
_____
_____
_____
_____
_____
_____

List some ideas for your speaking mantra?

_____
_____
_____
_____
_____
_____
_____
_____

Chapter Challenge:

What can you add to your talk to "dress it up"? What props or examples can you incorporate to make it more interesting?

Notes:

Notes:

CHAPTER NINE

Choose Your Food and Drink Wisely

"Work before eating, rest after eating. Eat not ravenously, filling the mouth gulp after gulp without breathing space." Maimonides

Have at least some food in your stomach before you speak. If you are hungry while making a presentation, there could be some unfortunate outcomes. If you are presenting while seated at a table, those on either side of you will hear every sound your body makes. Even if you are walking around, the audience may hear your stomach growl. You may also feel dizzy or lightheaded. Eating a small meal a few hours before your speech is ideal.

Carrying snacks in your car is a good way to prevent feeling hungry during a presentation. I learned this the hard way, after getting woozy during a talk. I made it through, and I don't think my audience noticed, but I promised myself it wouldn't happen again.

Watch what you eat and drink before you speak. Selecting the wrong items can have negative consequences. Following are some helpful hints on your best options.

Avoid milk, ice cream, cheese, alcohol, cold drinks and caffeine. Why? Dairy produces mucus, making your voice less resonant than you would like. You may also have to keep clearing your throat, which doesn't look or sound good to your audience. Room temperature beverages are best as cold drinks tend to constrict your throat.

Although you may feel that you need coffee to increase your energy level, too much coffee can make you feel jittery. Coffee peps you up, and you usually don't need additional more energy when you are speaking. Caffeine is dehydrating and leaves your larynx dry. (3) If you must drink coffee, drink decaf.

Water is a much better beverage because it helps to lubricate your vocal chords. Add a little lemon to keep them clear. Drink from a glass, not from a bottle. Why? Have you ever seen your face when you're drinking from a bottle? It's all scrunched up, which is not attractive. Keep yourself hydrated, making sure that water is easily accessible in case you need it.

Watch your sugar intake. You'll get a sugar rush, but then you'll have to deal with the sugar crash, which lasts a lot longer than the initial blast.

Alcohol is a no-no. You need to be sharp, and alcohol dulls the senses, causing you to slur your words or be unsteady on your feet. Spirits reduce your inhibitions, so you may utter inappropriate things. Even if you are the after- dinner speaker, and you feel that a glass of wine will help take the edge off, don't do it. It's best to save that drink for a celebration of your successful appearance once you get home.

When it comes to food choices, choose lean protein like fish or soy products over steak or a burger. Proteins stabilize your insulin level and provide fuel for mental focus. Vegetables are another good option. Carrot and celery sticks are easy to eat, even when your mouth is dry and you have knots in your stomach. Juicy vegetables like peppers and cherry tomatoes can also provide hydrating water to help keep you mentally sharp. (4)

Some clients will insist that you have a meal with them. When your host offers you food or drink, the polite response is to accept. However, if your client offers alcohol, simply explain that you prefer not to drink before you speak, and take them up on their offer after your presentation, if you are so inclined. You don't want to say or do anything that may damage your reputation.

Remember the Arabian Proverb which tells of the four things that don't come back, "the spoken word, the sped arrow, the past life, and the neglected opportunity." Watch your words carefully and you will open yourself to receive many more opportunities to speak.

Self-Assessment:

Why should you pay special attention to what you eat before a presentation?

_____
_____
_____
_____
_____
_____
_____

Why is it important to avoid alcohol before you speak?

_____
_____
_____
_____
_____
_____
_____

What are the best choices for food and beverage before a speech? Why?

_____
_____
_____
_____
_____
_____
_____

Chapter Challenge:

Choose a supportive friend to practice your speech on. Get constructive feedback. Ask for three things you did well, and one thing you can improve.

Notes:

Notes:

CHAPTER TEN

Dress Your Best for Speech Success

"What a strange power there is in clothing." Isaac Bashevis Singer

Give yourself enough time to get ready so that you look your best. When you look fabulous, you bolster your confidence and feel fantastic. Choose professional clothes that fit well. Invest in a full-length mirror so you can see your complete image before you take the stage. Dress at a level above that of your audience. If you are presenting at a conference where dress is casual or business casual, you may not have to wear an ultra-conservative suit, but you do want to make sure that you dress professionally. This will enhance your credibility.

Make sure your shoes are well-maintained and polished. If the weather is nasty, wear boots and carry your shoes in with you. Make sure that your shoes don't detract from the rest of your outfit; people will notice. If possible, check out the surface on which you'll be walking. If you're on a platform, make sure you don't have shoes that click and clack every time you take a step. The sound is annoying. If you are a woman, make sure you are wearing heels in which you can walk comfortably and naturally.

Whatever you are wearing, make sure that it fits properly. If you have either gained or lost weight, have your clothing tailored or purchase a few new pieces. Don't wait until you have reached your ideal weight before buying new clothes. People see you the way you look NOW, not when you lose those extra pounds.

If your style needs updating, ask a well-dressed friend to help you. Be adventurous - try on clothing that you wouldn't normally pick. Get out of your comfort zone and ask for honest opinions about what's working and what's not. You've probably watched a makeover show or two and seen how remarkable a "reveal" can be!

You may want to invest in an image consultant who will make sure you choose flattering colors and styles. It's astounding to see the impact that the right colors can have on your overall appearance. A few years ago, I had my "colors" done. The consultant gave me a business-card sized chart that I keep with me at all times.

Whenever I am buying clothes, I use the card to make sure they're in my color range. Make sure that you feel wonderful in any clothes you purchase. When you look and feel good in your clothes, you feel confident on stage. (5)

Whether you like it or not, people are judging you based on your appearance. You can make a positive first impression and start off strong. Or you can create a negative impression and have to work much harder to build your credibility.

> Whether you like it or not, people judge you based on your appearance. You can make a positive first impression and start off strong. Or you can create a negative impression and have to work much harder to build your credibility.

Here are some tips for choosing your outfit.

For women:

If your audience is casual or business casual, you have several options for outfits. You can choose a matched pantsuit, a solid colored jacket and trousers, a skirt and blouse, or trousers and a long-sleeved blouse. You never want to go sleeveless. No matter how impressive your arms look, a business presentation is not the time to show them off. As Image Consultant Danielle Turcola says, "The more skin you show, the less credibility you have."

For formal groups, a skirt suit or pant suit is a superb choice. Wear jewelry that doesn't make noise or is distracting. Err on the side of being conservative.

Watch your skirt length. When choosing a skirt, keep in mind that when you sit your skirt shortens three inches. According to The Image Resource Group (6) "to pinpoint the exact length that is both flattering and professional, stand up and make a circle with your two thumbs and index fingers and locate it around your kneecap. Any length at the circle, inside the circle, or lower than the circle is an appropriate length." When your skirt is too short, it draws attention away from you and your message.

Hair should be neat and combed. Focus on a sophisticated or conservative style. Don't have a style that is considered playful or too sexy. Make sure to wear makeup, proper undergarments, and hosiery. Again, check your reflection from the front and back in a full-length mirror.

For men

A casual look is much easier for men than women to achieve. Wear a button down shirt or a golf shirt with slacks made of blended wool or cotton. Make sure your clothes don't look as if you slept in them. Keep your shoes clean and polished. Details count.

When you're wearing a suit, make sure that it's tailored well. The Style Guy at "GQ" magazine says proper sleeve length is "about a half inch of shirt cuff showing below your jacket cuff, just as a half inch of shirt collar should show above your jacket collar." (7)

It's important to note that every man has one arm that is always longer than the other. This makes is necessary to measure each arm separately to properly determine the length of each suit sleeve. Arms should be relaxed at your sides for correct hemline placement. (7)

When your suit fits you well, you will be seen as a more credible, professional presenter, and you will also feel more confident because you know you look great!

Watch your use of cologne. You don't want the audience to smell you coming before they see you. Keep in mind that you may have people in the audience that are sensitive or allergic to fragrance so it's better not splash any on at all.

First impressions count.

Self-Assessment:

How should you dress for your presentations?

_____
_____
_____
_____
_____
_____

In what ways can a presenter improve their professional image?

_____
_____
_____
_____
_____
_____
_____

What does clothing say about a person?

_____
_____
_____
_____
_____
_____
_____

Chapter Challenge:

Now that you've outlined your speech, written it and practiced it, it's now time to give your speech to one of the organizations on your list. Know that you'll be GREAT!

Notes:

It's Now Up to You...

"There are three things to aim at in public speaking: First, to get into your subject, then to get your subject into yourself, then lastly , to get your subject into the heart of your audience"
Alexander Gregg

When you're first starting out, public speaking is scary business. Use the tips in this book to boost your self-assurance and your professional image. As a poised and confident speaker, you positively impact your career; no matter whether you want to be able to stand up and make a business presentation without making a fool of yourself, or you want to join the ranks of professional speakers. Use the ten concepts outlined in this book to captivate your audience with your skills, knowledge, and expertise.

To summarize the ten ideas, remember, above all else - if you fail to prepare, you prepare to fail. When you thoroughly know your speech, your confidence grows.

Don't memorize your talk. A memorized speech sounds canned and unnatural. Speak from your heart. You know your message and all you are doing is sharing your knowledge with your audience.

Look for the friendly faces to boost your self-esteem. Your audience wants to like you, and when you make them smile with your humor, they like you even more.

> **Don't strive for perfection. Go for excellence. There is a difference.**

Don't strive for perfection. Go for excellence. There is a difference.

Pausing adds drama and variety to your talk. Play with the pause. Never be afraid of moments of silence. Your audience will appreciate the opportunity you are giving them to keep pace with you.

Act confident and you'll feel confident. Give yourself a pep talk, stand tall, look forward, and walk with purpose. The audience will not see your nervousness.

When you appreciate your audience, they feel your sincerity and engage more fully with you.

Make sure that you are getting adequate rest on a daily basis, and most importantly before you talk. Get up early so you can take your time, collect your thoughts and get to the venue in a calm, cool and collected manner.

Choose the food and drink that support you and your talk. Eating a couple of hours before your talk is ideal.

Finally, make sure you look terrific for your talk. When you know you look good, your confidence soars, and you'll go out and rock your presentation.

There you have it! Ten tips you need to overcome your public speaking anxiety. Go ahead, get out there, and speak.

It's time for you to shine!

Self-Assessment:

What is your biggest takeaway from these ten tips?

_____
_____
_____
_____
_____
_____
_____
_____

What will you do, starting today, to improve your speaking skills?

_____
_____
_____
_____
_____
_____
_____
_____

How will you put these suggestions to use in your upcoming speaking events?

_____
_____
_____
_____
_____
_____
_____
_____

Chapter Challenge:

It's time to celebrate! Write down everything you've done well during this training program. Consider each and every improvement a victory and congratulate yourself. YOU DID IT!

_____
_____
_____
_____
_____
_____
_____
_____
_____
_____
_____
_____
_____
_____
_____
_____
_____
_____
_____
_____

Notes:

Notes:

References:

(1) http://statisticbrain.com/fear-of-public-speaking-statistics/

(2) http://www.merriam-webster.com/dictionary/memorize

(3) http://www.livestrong.com/article/539272-foods-that-are-unhealthy-for-your-vocal-cords/#ixzz2KYTFy3lE

(4) http://www.livestrong.com/article/142925-foods-that-reduce-speech-anxiety/

(5) http://www.wikihow.com/Reduce-Stress-Before-Giving-a-Speech

(6) http://professionalimagedress.com/women_skirt.htm

(7) http://www.ehow.com/info_8697636_correct-length-mans-suit-jacket.html#ixzz2MWQDSUwJ

Acknowledgements:

I want to express my deepest gratitude to Westside Advanced Toastmasters who provided valuable insight and feedback for this book. Thank you Betsy McKinney, Marie Monago, Maryanne Petranek, Sherry Watts and Rick Winrod. I appreciate the time and effort that each of you put into my book!

A very special thank you goes to Linda Harvey, who took it upon herself to thoroughly and expertly edit this book. Linda, you have a true gift for revising, reworking, and rearranging the written word, and your talent and skill truly transformed this book. Thank you, I am so grateful for you!

I also want to thank my friend Chris King who introduced me to Toastmasters International, and inspired me to become a speaker, writer and entrepreneur.

Finally, thank you to my wonderful husband, Scott, who supports me through all the madness of a speaking and writing career. I could not do this without you, Scott, and I love you with all my heart. Thank you!

About Lisa Ryan

My life was dramatically altered in 1987 when I participated in a Dale Carnegie course entitled, "Public Speaking and Effective Human Relations" (now simply known as the Dale Carnegie Course.)

From the moment I discovered the power of a professional presentation, I felt a calling to become a professional speaker. I created a list of my goals and "Become a professional speaker" ranked #2 on a list of eighty-nine items. "Write a book" was third. ("Buy a house" was #1, in case you were curious.)

My professional speaking goal languished on the back burner for many years as I embarked on a successful sales career. Granted, I was conducting training programs and continuing education classes in my job, but I was always presenting "other people's stuff." I yearned to be a speaker in my own right.

When my medical sales career came to a crashing halt (via a group conference call where twelve of us were let go at the same time), I decided to pursue the dream I had held for more than twenty years and become an inspirational speaker.

I wrote this book to help people who want to improve their speaking ability, but don't feel that they have the confidence or skills to move forward.

As Founder and Chief Appreciation Strategist at Grategy®, I am having a blast working with corporations, associations, and non-profits. The theme of my talks is to inspire my clients to discover the power of gratitude for stronger relationships, improved health and increased profits by leveraging employee and customer engagement, retention and recognition strategies.

Since the time my sales career came to its dramatic end, I have written two printed books: *The Upside of Down Times: Discovering the Power of Gratitude* and *With Excellence*, and three e-books. My proven gratitude technology (Grategy) is featured in the movie, "The Keeper of the Keys," where I co-star with Jack Canfield, author of *Chicken Soup for the Soul*, John Gray of *Men are from Mars/Women are from Venus*, and Marci Shimoff from *The Secret*. In "The Gratitude Experiment," I co-star with Bob Proctor, Dr. John Demartini and Mary Morrissey, all of whom were in the 2006 movie sensation, "The Secret."

Please contact me if you'd like more information on bringing me to your next event: www.grategy.com, lisa@grategy.com , or 216-225-8027

Thank you, I appreciate you!

Other Books from Lisa Ryan

The Upside of Down Times: Discovering the Power of Gratitude. http://amzn.to/NjNs06
Uncover four areas in your life that can be transformed by using the power of appreciation. Entertaining, inspiring and includes plenty of activities so you can get started right away.

Keeper of the Keys: Taking the Hell Out of Self-Help (movie)
http://lisaryanonline.com
Laid off from his job, his house in foreclosure, his engagement broken, Michael Walden was having a bad day. This film follows Michael's incredible journey to finding the keys to a happy and successful life. Also starring Jack Canfield (*Chicken Soup for the Soul*), Marci Shimoff (*The Secret*) and John Gray (*Men are from Mars…*)

The Gratitude Experiment (movie)
http://www.thegratitudeexperiment.com/index.html
If you liked "The Secret," you'll love "The Gratitude Experiment." A variety of world-renowned experts share research, stories, and anecdotes on the immense power of appreciation in our life. You'll also get to hear the humorous answers that children give when asked about thankfulness.

Thank You Notes: Your 30 Days of Gratitude Workbook *http://bit.ly/Opzmb4*
Take the challenge. For the next 30 days, discover all the ways you can harness the power of gratitude

With Excellence *http://bit.ly/YK6ssP*
A compilation of stories to help you create a life of excellence.

Mind Power *http://bit.ly/WnNYBK*
Enjoy my gift to you just for visiting my site

How to Keep in touch

Questions for the Author?
Email me at lisa@grategy.com

Want to receive your own Gratitude Thought for the Week?
http://www.grategy.com

Would you like to learn more about Toastmasters International?
http://www.toastmasters.org/

Thank You!

I appreciate you!

CPSIA information can be obtained
at www.ICGtesting.com
Printed in the USA
LVOW09s0220010218
564881LV00019B/693/P

9 781484 038154